SELECTED POEMS

SELECTED POEMS

THOMAS GRISSOM

SUNSTONE PRESS

SANTA FE

Sunstone books may be purchased for educational, business, or sales promotional use.
For information please write: Special Markets Department, Sunstone Press,
P.O. Box 2321, Santa Fe, New Mexico 87504-2321.

Design › R. Ahl
Printed on acid-free paper
∞
eBook 978-1-61139-642-3

Library of Congress Cataloging-in-Publication Data

Names: Grissom, Thomas, 1940- author.
Title: Selected poems / Thomas Grissom.
Description: Santa Fe, NM : Sunstone Press, [2021] | Summary: "Lyric poems
  of uncompromising truth and honesty selected by the author from his
  previous collections as among those he would most want to preserve"--
  Provided by publisher.
Identifiers: LCCN 2021050000 | ISBN 9781632933652 (paperback) | ISBN
  9781611396423 (epub)
Subjects: LCGFT: Poetry.
Classification: LCC PS3607.R577 S45 2021 | DDC 811/.6--dc23/eng/20211117
LC record available at https://lccn.loc.gov/2021050000

WWW.SUNSTONEPRESS.COM
SUNSTONE PRESS / POST OFFICE BOX 2321 / SANTA FE, NM 87504-2321 /USA
(505) 988-4418

DEDICATION

For all who have ever thought a poem.

CONTENTS

From *One Spring More*

From *Journal Entries*

From *Neither Here Nor There*

PREFACE

These are among the poems, going forward, that I would most want to preserve. I have selected them from previous collections according to my own assessment of merit and for the special place they occupy still in my thoughts and feelings. They are the ones I am most pleased, and even in some cases surprised, to have written. They are not arranged according to any conscious scheme or with any particular preconceived order in mind. They are meant to be thought of individually and to stand alone on their own. For anyone who insists on imposing a thematic order, I can only suggest that running through them all is a constant thread of individual truth and honesty. Stephen Crane remarked early in his career that he liked his little poems better than his fiction. The reason, he confessed, was that in the poems he allowed himself to say what he truly believed. It should be so of all lyric poetry and is a cogent recommendation of how to approach these poems.

Thomas Grissom
OTHER
TRUTHS
Poems

HIDDEN DREAMS

I dreamed a poem unwritten
In thoughts that lay unborn
Conceived in troubled sleep
Dispersed by light of morn;
Then struggled through the day
To find those thoughts once more
Unable to recall
The paths I'd walked before;
And truths that night concealed
From day's bright scrutiny
Stay hidden in my mind
To shape my destiny.

THOUGHTS ARE POEMS

I was going to write a poem
Out of words that never came
And the thoughts that I was thinking
Just fell like April rain
To be soaked up by the garden
Of memories in my mind
Where they nurture other thoughts
That I will use another time...

SIMPLE PLEASURES
(Sunday Afternoon)

I write simple words
in simple lines
on yellow scraps of paper.
Does some truth
come peeking through these thoughts,
or does it even matter?
Is there something here
that might not be said
unless I took the time,
or do I just record
what others all may know
and waste the time
I could have had for living?
But then,
what would living be
without these simple pleasures
of the mind?

SHADES OF BLUE

i)

Azure blue
bright desert skies
shimmering tears
in sad blue eyes
august now has come and gone
with april, june and july
but the sadness in my heart
still lingers on and on...

ii)

Sunrise and sunset
And all the times between
Slowly pile upon each other
To make my days now seem
Like endless hours of torture
That creep so slowly by
While I wrestle with my thoughts
About the countless reasons why.

iii)

There are clouds in the sky
That block the sun
Casting shadows on the mountains
Since you've gone
And days that are an endless string
Of hours dragging by
As I sit and contemplate
The complicated reasons why.

SCHIZOPHRENOS

I have forgotten what I am—
Uncertain I ever knew—
And I search in vain for meaning
Among all I thought was true;

A future ripe with promise
Has escaped into the past;
Each moment slips by fearful
That the next might be my last;

I reach and grope for comfort
That is only found within
To find my faltering efforts
Always reflected back again;

This drama forms the essence
Of the childhood times of me
And life's most threatening puzzle
Of what could and would I be.

UNKNOWN ROADS

As I drive along these unknown roads
The cars all seem to swerve and vie
To get around and pass me by,
With drivers impatient of one (such as I)
Who does not seem to know his way.
It is the same, also, for me
Along life's unfamiliar paths
As the lonely hours of each day
And the silent seasons slip away
Impatient to be done with one
For whom each change is a thing so slow
That he doesn't seem to know his way
Or even where he meant to go.

PUZZLES

Can I be quite as bad
as you have led me
to believe?
Could anyone,
ever?
If not,
why would you think so?

And if you're right
why can't I see
it too,
or are we looking
at different pieces
of the same puzzle?

All the pieces will be needed
to solve the riddle;
not one can be hoarded
if we would ever know
the truth.

If any piece is missing
it will not
be found
by looking
in the dark
or made to fit
in the puzzle
upside down.

The greatest danger
is that one of us
will tire of this game
before the puzzle
is complete,
or see just enough
of it unfinished
to guess
the ending wrong.

As I recall
we never were
very good
at puzzles.

TO DIANA

The relationship of man
and woman tenuous
at best

at worst precarious
was in the case
of you

and me the only source
of my salvation
amidst

the perils of extinction
such distinction
should

not go unheralded in a
world of failures
we were

one of the success
stories of the
age.

OTHER TRUTHS

The mind seeks beauty in all the eyes behold
And listens for the truths that nature told—
Yet pauses for a moment now and then
Before a truth it cannot comprehend:
Sees the hurtling falcon's murderous plunge;
Hears the snarling leopard's deadly lunge;
Feels the numbing wastes of frozen lands;
Smells the bloated death in desert sands;
Finds it in the anguished cries of man
Shackled to his fleeting mortal span,
Driven by his consciousness to try
To fathom multitudes of reasons why—
Then wonders why a God who made the beauty
Would make these other truths so hard to see.

HELEN

Is this that which launched a thousand ships
And drew the mighty Greeks to Ilium's shore;
For ten years stirring clash of arms across
The Trojan Plains to end old Priam's line;
Inspiring the epic strains of Homer's verse
Creating for all times the sounds of poetry?
These sagging withered breasts are hardly fit
To succor worms. The wrinkled skin, the faded
Hair betray no echoes of the past.
Now only death desires these barren loins
That once lured lovers to the nuptial couch
And promised nights that time could never dim.
No, this creased and aging form now palsied
And enfeebled is not what stirred men's passions
And compelled the poet to sing. This is just
An empty shell, the debris of a life
Whose essence lies beyond the faded past;
This is but the blunted instrument
That carved a scratch on anonymity.

AFFIRMATION AND DEDICATION

He locked his heart in a silver box
And wrapped his mind in golden chains
And placed them on the altar
Of a grand and stately church;
Beneath the years of fear and gloom,
Beside the moldy, mildewed pages
Of the greatest story ever told
And the world's all-time best seller;
Sheltered from the anguish and the torment
        of the ages
Muffled by the thick stone walls and the sounds
        of sacred hymns
Sung by souls in praise of God created
        in their image;
In a place where the sun never shines,
Where the soft, spring winds never blow;
In a place where nothing happens at all.

REFLECTIONS

Brooding deep within himself
He views the landscapes of his mind
And sorts out childhood memories
From scenes of harsher times;

And hears the peals of laughter
That swept those sunlit plains
Fade from the grasp of memory
Replaced by cries of pain;

As did the child become the man
So changed his world along the way
Transformed from brightest colors
To shades of somber gray;

Until at last the darkness
Engulfs him all around;
His eyes close for the last time;
He hears no further sound;

But embarked on his last journey
To rest beneath the sod
He leaves it now to others
To contemplate a God.

CAMELOT—THE IMPOSSIBLE DREAM
(*RFK*)

I recall with grief the moment when the bullet struck
        im down
With its snapping, frightening, sickening, fateful,
        prophesying sound
That dashed his hopes with ours a crumpled heap upon
        the ground;
The chaos and the tumult of the startled, swirling crowd
Drowning out the promised hopes of what might still
        have been
In the numbing realization of what now would never be;

—Somewhere in the land a lady said with dirgeful glee,
"Well, that will make an honest man of him."—

        She spoke for all those honest men
        Who hate and seethe and loathe
        And fight to keep us free
        To murder dreams and dreamers
        Of visions yet to be.

ANTIQUE TRUTHS

I stopped by the antique fair
To reminisce and view the wares,
Every object old and worn,
The luster gone that time had shorn,
The only test for being there
The toll of years that each had born,
No concern at all for usefulness
Then or now—junk some might call it—
Yet not exactly junk somehow
To those who came to look and learn
What antique truths they could discern
In peering safely back through time
And holding firmly to the grasp
Of the certainty of the past.

ALL THE WORLD'S A POEM

"There is one God and the Earth is His prophet."
—Robinson Jeffers

All the world's a poem
Printed on the earth
Where God the Poet writes
With majesty His verse

In the splendid truths
That simple nature told
To minds that search for beauty
In all the eyes behold;

And when a verse obscure
We strive to understand
Seek the final meaning
Within the mind of man;

For if unconvinced
Why each verse is true
At least we can be certain
That the Poet knew.

CYCLES

Rolling wave on rolling wave
Comes tumbling into shore
Booming loudly o'er the land
The sea's majestic roar.

Driven on by wind and wave
And calmed at last by land
The mounting seas come surging forth
To crash upon the sand.

Muffled murmurings of long ago
When life began beneath the sea;
Distant sounds from ages past
And of things still yet to be.

Written in this ageless cycle
Summarized for all to know
Is the essence of the universe
And nature's endless flow.

THE LAST WHOOPING CRANE
(*At Bosque del Apache*)

He stalks among the sandhills
a relic from the past;
his solitary presence,
a portent for the future,
marks him now the last
of a species perched precariously
on the edge of extinction
as the passenger pigeon
and the ivory bill before,
soon to be a footnote
in a text on evolution.
The ghost white form goes gliding
through the reeds along the marsh
spearing fish in the shallows
like a prehistoric savage,
one bright eye always cocked
and intent upon the prey,
the wind gently rustling
the delicate feathery spray,
water dripping from the beak
sending ripples through the pond
like memories of times gone by
when other whoopers waded there.
Who knows what is lost
when at last he is no more;
can we measure it,
and how could we ignore
his going till that time

when by then it was too late
to register any change
in the species' final fate?
They are but empty questions,
more than we can comprehend,
this measure of the meaning
of a life form's final end.

THE FLOCK

The gulls
swarming, swirling
shrieking, shrilling
turning, twisting
twining, throbbing
probing, prying
pressing, pulsing
a raucous chorus of cacophonous cries
frantic pleadings of urgent expectancy
a swelling cloud of white on blue
rising from the beach
like dancing scraps of paper
swept aloft on sudden gusts
flapping, floating
flaring, fluttering
sweeping, swooping
settling, standing
facing squarely in the wind
staring calmly at the sea
preening, peering
passive, patient
the gulls.

POINT OF VIEW
The Poets: the Poets lie too much—Thus Spoke Zarathustra

I would that I had written my poems
Or even one
Than all else I have done in life
Or left undone;

And I would have been troubled by life
Than to have sailed complacently through
For nights still separate the days
And thorns will grow where roses do.

I would that I thought bitter thoughts
Or one or two
Than all the sweeter things in life
I didn't do;

For I have come by that to know
Much more of truth than I redeem
From all the pleasantries of life
That never are quite what they seem.

IMMORTALITY

The desert skies will be my shroud
Its sands will clothe my bones
Its birds will sing me lullabies
When fore'er it is my home;

And I will lie deep in its quiet
While immortal time drifts by
As the universe unfolds each night
In the starlit desert sky;

My atoms linked with all that's been
And all that's yet to be
Will serve me well enough, I think,
For immortality.

THE POLITICIAN AND THE AGING ACTOR

The Politician greeted the Aging Actor on a stage
Shadowed by towering memorials and magnificent
        buildings of state—

Said the Politician:
I told them of the need to preserve the dignity of man,
        to strive for human rights;
To cleanse the environment for our children and to gird
        for a future of limited growth;
But they did not want to hear: to be believed
Such words must come from the mouth of a great leader.

Answered the Aging Actor:
They are greedy and do not want to know the truth;
And a nation of greedy men does not breed
        great leaders;
But they are gullible and I can act the part: tell them
What they want to hear while doing what is necessary;
Give them what they desire, and if they destroy
        themselves
At least I will glory in my last great role.

At the final curtain the two took their bows
To a standing ovation from the crowd
And glowing acclaim from the critics.

Thomas Grissom

ONE
SPRING MORE

Poems

THE GIFT SHE EARLY GAVE TO ME

The darkly dappled duns of spring muffle a
Woman's weaning sobs that stain with alkaline
Lace the mirrored masks reflected round
Her speechless sorrow, shrieking still across
The gape of gnawing years to mold my mind
In moribund pain—perhaps to strike me dumb
For silence softly spent in soul's repast
When lilting-laughtered games with shadowed moths
Through sweet magnolia scents would not suffice.
By brighter bells she spoke the earthly coarsened
Tones that tolled the fates of decent folk
To one alive in less imperfect worlds and
Shaped me from the common clay that crumbles
Under grinding heel in disarray
Unprincipled, till hardened to insensate
Stone it finally breaks and shatters in
Discordant sounds the senses suffer to
Escape in absolution lightly laved.
And spirits flowed from fecund fields and lands
That lavished servitude upon those hapless
Held in bondage ill of their own choosing,
Who best the farrowed fetters chained them knew
Blankly without hate or love that lately
Lonely voices raise to fearful ears,
To infuse my soul with fertile seeds that one
Day grew to claim the soil of thought and deed

With noisy clamor out of context like
The child the sounds it sends to show the world
The life it briefly reckons then rescinds.
With ever steady touch she gentled febrile
Brow against the tumult raged within, till
Calmed in contemplation upon seas of
Tranquil truths I cherished secrets of
The heavens reflected in those depths, then peering
Deeper in my languorous labor found
The image everywhere the same my own,
And storms that tossed the troubled seas then brought
To life a sweeter taste it had not known
And swept me from my task ashore to stroll
Again in light and dappled duns of springs
The wanning winters wield, now proudly mantled
By the cloak of years that gentler sends
The knell of sheltered sounds that gives at last
To her the gift she early gave to me.

THE GOLDEN ANNIVERSARY

i) Patriarchal

The graying head is now sometimes bowed as
The stooped form moves slowly on its accustomed
Rounds between house and yard and barn,
Patiently doing whatever he can do,
No more than a memory of years past.
The pastures grow taller between mowings
Than before, the leaves pile up on the roof, the lawn
Sprouts dandelions—for in these he is at the mercy
Of others. The fierce blue eyes are dimmed
And grope in shadows. The still powerful shoulders
Tell a quarter of a lifetime and his best years
Spent on crutches, in pain. At times
The hands grow frustrated, the expression
Resigned. But the face is clear
The sharp nose and stern features still
Softened by the easy smile of one
Who has always viewed the compromises of life
As bargains of his own making. There is no bitterness
And little regret. In this lies his strength.

In his life he has found some answers
Though some remain a mystery that like most
He does not easily confess or simply no longer
Ponders, content at last to leave that to others;
He will live out the remaining days at peace

In his mind—it is little enough to ask. Evenings
By the fire where before he would read he sits in
Drawing darkness and dreams, remembering a life
    lived
Simply and honestly, doing whatever had to be done
Not intentionally hurting anyone and mostly unaware
When he did; those who recall remember him as
A friend. He thinks too of days to come and
Things he will yet do before he is finished. For
He will not "go gentle into that good night," but
When he must he will depart life as he lived it
Doing all that is expected of him. And in this
Final measure he will be missed, his legacy
Secure in the hearts and minds of those he loved.

ii) Matriarchal

For a moment the wistful eyes hold a dreamy
Far-away look a smile as quickly dispels
That lights the still pleasing face—
In the old photographs she is pretty, and though
By nature disparaging she would deny it,
We too could see what he had seen
Who after all these years still feels the same;
Now the wispy, graying hair frames a face
Figured like a tapestry with the images
Of a lifetime and the lives around which it was
Woven unselfishly, of unfulfilled aspirations—
In the early years, the children and the house
She filled with warmth and love, quietly enjoying
Their triumphs and successes even as she suffered
The defeats and failures she often could not
Understand, giving to each one in turn something
Of herself and finding there something in return.
She saw her duty clearly and simply and carried it out
Stubbornly through the frailty and the sickness

Complaining no more than most and less
Than she might have of a certain bitterness
And the youth she felt slipping away; their
Needs were simple and they never measured
Happiness by those things she found lacking.
His conscience through the years, she later
Shared his burden of pain and infirmity, reckoning
Then her needs by his who now the world must
View through her eyes, and found at last
A fulfillment of children and grandchildren
And the satisfaction of a lifetime stretching out
Behind her in the union of half a century—
Her duty she might reply, but love to us the same
Just as surely by any other name.

GOING BLIND

Sometimes you can notice it
By the curious way he doesn't look straight
        at you, but askance,
As though he wished to view things from a
        slightly different slant—
Out of the corner of his eye, or the corner
        of his mind, the way
One would at night in looking at a star
Or at some other thing too faint to see, or
        know, straight away;
The center of the retina has deteriorated, the
        images falling there a darkened
Blur of jumbled lines too tangled and distorted
To discern. They have a term for it, these
Medical men who believe that names confer
A measure of understanding: senile macula
        retinitis
And it says nothing. He has his own name
        for it—
It is called going blind, and he understands it
In a way they never will—the sickening sense
        of panic in a
World of early twilights and lingering dawns, the
Fiercely proud spirit helplessly dependent; then
Gradual realization and utter finality. In all,
Ten siblings were born—one died a child, another

A young man of pneumonia, a third of early
          senility—
The others after sixty-five have all had this
          affliction; now
Three generations of children and grandchildren
Await a fate woven in the twisted strands
          of nucleic acids:
For my part, I shall miss the colors and
The faces of children. But I have seen these
And memory serves me well. More, I would
Crave the sight of words printed boldly on
          smooth pages, for which
The eyes are handmaiden to the mind. Does
This prophecy foretold make each new sunset
Ever more beautiful? It is not possible:
Born with the knowledge of our death, life
          is not sweeter.

I MET A POET

When I was a youth, a poet
Spoke to me, who said:
Poetry is next to godliness—
Beside mathematics and philosophy
And science—
Each thing that we learn
But a tiny part of a greater whole
Expanding without limit
To encompass all knowledge, the universe
And ourselves—
But I paid his words no heed,
Turning from the tortuous twists of poetry
To the plainer paths of science
And spent my years in futile search
Of truth
Ever vanishing into metaphor,
Until lost and confused
I met another poet, who said—
If you would find yourself
Look with the poet's eyes.

HALF-FINISHED POEMS

I have a stack of half-finished poems
Good beginnings gone awry—most
Beyond repair; beyond redemption, all;
The pen stymied in mid-verse, something
Wrong with each right from the start—
The words flowing out too quickly
Overran the thought, or else labored over
So long the spark extinguished
Before it could be fanned to flames.
Now they lie tucked away in a sheath,
And tucked away in my mind,
Where they will not let me rest
But torment me with their failure
Like stillborn babes, or the anguish
Of a child the parent struggles to save;
Others see the poems but not the labor
And so few words, they think,
Could not cost that much—
They give great pleasure these words of ours
But exact in payment a price of pain
Equal to their bliss.

MONTANA MUSE

Almost overlooked
        in the pale
                moonlight
a small
        hand-lettered sign
                in the window
of the Meagher
        County News
                announcing
"An afternoon
        Of Montana Poetry
                at Chico Hot Springs"
with the date,
        the names
                of a dozen poets
and a special
        invitation for
                certain strangers
like myself
        to join in,
                but unable to
I pass on by,
        later in the
                dark of my room
pleased that
        poetry still lives
                in quiet little

out of the way
        places,
                in the quiet
out of the way
        places
                of the mind.

BREAKDANCING

Every corner
        and the bus stops
                in between
a stage of
        spinning symmetries
                and the choreographed
contortions
        of sinewy shapes
                that spell out
exuberance for life
        and the exultant
                jubilation
of a people
        discovering
                art.

A FULL-TIME OCCUPATION

Writing poems is a full-time occupation;
I don't mean that it pays, and besides
I'd only give the money away, it's best
Done for free; in truth I could not
Do otherwise with no regard to pay
Without dying just a bit and being
Less than the person I still somehow
Need to be. No, it's the evolution
Of the thing, I mean, the ideas come
At the least expected times and in
The least expected ways all bright and full
Of promise and truth that too long neglected
Is never quite the same yet seized upon
Keeps on growing to become more than
At first it seemed, revealing truths we did
Not know we knew, "No surprise for
The writer, no surprise for the reader,"
Said Frost, then fixed in thought keeps worrying
Suggesting little changes to my mind
Each one tried against the others to find
That one just right not to disappoint
Till finally set aside to return now and
Then and learn if truth will bear retelling;
Meanwhile the faucets drip the shelves will go
Unfinished, she pretends she does not care
Though at times I know she must; the love

She gives softens here and there a line
That otherwise too harsh might sound for what
Was really meant and harm my purpose; for
The rest they are my own as they must be
It will not work another way. And when
At times my object is the more efficient
Means to kill, though others will not call
It that and say instead to keep the peace,
And anguished faces haunt my mind till I
Grow weary with the world and yearn heartfelt
For other realms which only mind may know,
At length some thought becomes my solace made
A poem, then all else I gladly set
Aside for this my full-time occupation.

ALL MY FRIENDS

The knock came gently at the open door;
"Sir," the young man spoke, "I didn't mean
To interrupt . . ." "Yes, well I am quite busy
Just now," the man responded, "but no, no come
On in," he said and rose to make him welcome;
The tiny office was cluttered with stacks on
Stacks of books, and papers he'd been writing
Scattered across the desk, the words in places
Lined through and written above, some more
        than once
In exacting labor of love. He cleared a chair
Of books and bade him sit; outside the window
A clinging mist hung dangling from the tips of
Jeweled boughs. The man's gaze briefly turned
Back toward the words that he'd been writing;
"My uncle Josh asked me to call," the other
Hastened to explain. "When he learned that
This would be my school, he told me you had
Come here and that I should stop by and say
Hello . . . You do remember Josh and Sarah?"
"Why yes, of course," he interrupted," I should
Have known at once—the freckles and the reddish
Hair—and how are Josh and Sarah? Tell
Me all about them, and about yourself," he
Smiled. "They're fine as near as anyone can
Tell. You know Josh, he's hard to read; never

Complains—just does whatever must be done.
Both mighty sorry to see you go, that much
I know for sure; Josh told me they all were.
Josh says he'll probably never leave. Been
There now for almost thirty years and says
He'll likely stay the rest. I don't suppose
He ever will retire. He told me though to
Tell you that he understands." The young man
Blurted out everything he'd thought of saying.
In his eyes there was the eager look of
Youth the man had come to know and like
In faces all around him. The only hope that's
Left for us, he sometimes told himself. He
Felt anew the empty longing of homesickness
The way he had those first few times he'd severed
Ties and struck out on his own. He didn't
Miss the work. He'd done it for the money
Much longer than he meant to, and for the
Others, and the loyalty and the friendships,
Until he could not do it anymore. No,
It was only the people that he missed, the ones
Like Josh who understood—him best of all—and
Nothing changed between them. They sat in
      awkward
Silence. "Sir," the youth at length broke in,
"Is something wrong?" "No," he said, "I'm sorry,
It's just that I was thinking—how ironic and
Strange it is—that all my friends build bombs."

ON VIEWING THE IMPRESSIONISTS

i)
Quiet serious Monet
discussing art with Pissarro
at the café Guerbois or
the scoffing sensitive Renoir,
more likely listening
to Zola or Degas
with Sisley
and the ill-fated Bazille,
escaping to the country
to paint in
sumptuous floods of light the
short choppy strokes and bright daubs
of color—
too much garish color, they cried—
arrayed separately
on the canvas for the eye
to combine in scenes
of the only
truth he saw
—unacceptable for the Salon, they ruled,
no substance nothing
of the mind's eye—
in images blurred like
captured motion or a world
taking form
to as quickly fade from view

—not truly paintings at all,
they argued, too unreal
merely impressions—
yes, that was it
impressions
of a reality
ever shrinking
to exactly fit
these frames.

ii)
Explaining it all
years later to the five sons
Pissarro the astute
elder and many ways their leader
—a man worth consulting, said
Cezanne, and something like God himself—
who understood Monet
and the new Impressionism
not impressions
but reality itself depicted
as the senses
in *plein-air* colors
and softly smeared perceptions,
taking his lead from
the new Heraclitus but holding
to the clearer colors
and surer shapes of his early years
—you are a great blunderer, Sir,
wrote Zola,
you are an artist that I like—
to fashion his own reality,
not of forms
but the feelings
captured on each canvas.

iii)
Renoir who
scoffed at theories
painting was for pleasure
—if it didn't amuse me
then I shouldn't paint, he said—
found in fragile colors
and softly muted shapes that
display the delicate touch
striving for a time
with his friend Monet
after the new realism, then
tiring, rejected it
for the tender
sensuous faces of
women and children,
to paint reality
peering
demurely back.

iv)
Sisley at Marley
Bazille's *Beach at Sainte Adresse*
the triumphs went
unnoticed—one
neglected, the
other a soldier's
grave—impressions
of the reality
of us
all.

POPPA

He dogged my footsteps throughout
The city
                past the booksellers' stalls
Along the quais to a good café on
The Place St-Michel
                                the shadowy
Barrel-chested figure hands thrust
Into pockets head bowed graying
Hair and beard deepening winter's
Chill
        through the Luxembourg Gardens
Past Gertrude Stein's and 113 rue
Notre-Dame-des-Champs to the bustling
Closerie des Lilas
                                all traces
Have vanished
                            at 74 rue du
Cardinal Lemoine a discotheque
Replaces the sawmill, the voices
Of the charmed circle strangely
Silent at 27 rue de Fleurus
                                    only
The books survive and the few
Truths
                was it the early ones
When he first got lucky full of
Raw exuberance for life or the last
Ones wiser more compassionate and

Revealing
                    and the one about this
Place in the early years many ways
Closest to the truth
                              I caught a
Glimpse in the Jeu de Paume, the
Figure hunched intently before a canvas
Studying Cezanne to learn about
Writing
                        and in a clean well-lighted
Café the saucers stacked high pouring
Over yesterday's words to see if they
Were still true
                          once during dinner
At the Polidor listening and thinking
About what he wanted to do with
Conversations
                        nowhere yet everywhere
The watchful figure
                          among the crowds
On windswept streets and lovers in the
Gardens, in the cafes and the shops—
Anywhere there was life, that truth he
Found here and made his own—
                                      life and
Death and courage
                          summer and winter
And spring
                        and always the promise
Of another spring whispered from every
Stone and gray-green chestnuts beside
The Seine—courage for our time.

THE BALLAD OF BOBBIE'S BUCKEYE BAR
(*For GWS*)
With Apologies to Robert W. Service

From out of the desert they came by two's
In their drab gray government cars
In search of a glass of ice cold brew
At Bobbie's Buckeye Bar.

They spent their days below the ground
In tunnels men had made
The reasons hushed, though the rumor going round
Said they did it for the shade.

The sun now spent hung low in the slack
A bulging bloodshot eye
Peering aslant at that clapboard shack
Where this night a woman would try.

The moon rose up in the east pale gold
To shine on the scene below
Where in years to come the tale would be told
Of how Slim had just said no.

There was Shorty and Slim, the others and Rojo
And they came with a thirst to quench
But they reckoned without this gal named Flo
Who some say was a winsome wench.

She took an immediate hankering to Slim
And joined them at the bar
Taking her place in the space by him
This fair-haired desert star.

She touched his cheek and twirled his hair
And gently rubbed his back
And tried to get him to follow her there
To her room at the rear of the shack.

She nuzzled his neck and nipped his ear
And whispered things to him
That were spoken too low for the others to hear
She meant them only for Slim.

She looked in his eyes and stroked his chest
To the others it was more than clear
What they would do away from the rest
In the dark of her room at the rear.

She leaned right over to give him a peek
At a bosom that amply showed
Hers was no game of hide and seek
But a gift she freely bestowed.

She talked to him in a constant purr
Of the things that they would do
And of how if he would follow her
She could make him feel like new.

But through it all this hero just stood
And slowly sipped his beer
And thought of how she would be good
And wished that he wasn't there.

And even today in the Buckeye Bar
The patrons tell this tale
Of the tall dark man in the government car
To whom Flo couldn't make a sale.

Till when at last he turned to leave
There was not a dry eye in the place
The restraint of this fellow they couldn't believe
And tears wet every face.

He paused there a moment to slip a ten
In the center of Flo's brassiere
And caught the tremor of quivering chin
As she whispered in his ear.

And those who said they could hear the words
She spoke so soft and mellow
Swear that what they thought they heard
Was a sad, "So long, big fellow."

MOTES

The awning
left
a space

that sunlight
filled
about which

a demanding
woman
complained her

table heaped
with
food but

another across
the
way deferred

saying there
were
worse things

than sunlight
in
her eyes.

HEED THE VOICES OF ANGER

Whereto the runes of reason:
With them Socrates conquered the Dionysian
        spirit and, disillusioned,
Athens pointed to distant decline;
Lucretius composed for troubled minds but
        Rome unsoothed
Plunged the world to darkness;
Briefly like a meteor the Age of Reason lit up
        the western world—
Voltaire poured out his heart exhausted
In the folly of empire; and we but a passing
        phase to
Something else too ominous to contemplate—
At such times heed the voices of anger, the
        cries of
Caring, passionate poets too full
Of love for restraint—Euripides, Nietzsche,
        Thoreau, Jeffers—
Their pages stained with angry tears;
Our world smolders like a buried ember
        needing only
a breath of air and we numbed
Silence our fears and speak of baseball and
        politics and greed—
Let us raise a shout of anger!

ECCO HOMO

The slight little man with the nervous
Stomach and weak eyes,
To those few who inquired deferential to
A fault
Yet railing mightily against his demons
Through
Nine volumes wrenched from the depths
Of his solitude—
I am so completely alone, he would write,
Then—
Ariadne, I love you—and a date with
Madness—
What price this genius that gives our
Souls such pleasure—
What price Faulkner's suffering
Camus' godless anguish
Nietzsche's madness
To give our hearts such hope?

FALKLANDS

It is winter and war has come to
These islands;
Across storm-tossed seas corrupt Britannia
Strutting vaingloriously
One final moment in the sun sends warships
Against petty little dictators
The sons of honest folk in the balance;
No honor here—only equal wrongs—
America which neither side could oppose
Heaps rhetoric from afar upon graves
Of Argentine youth—
As a war it is of no real consequence
Merely a minor skirmish,
More penguins than people will perish,
An ad for Exocets and Entendards and
Good for the world's economy, more jobs
For French farmers—
Can we ever hope to build these weapons
Without using them?
No one should believe it.

A CHILD'S METAPHOR

One
tiny
drop
of
rain
after
another
through this graying mist,
in spring
the rivers overflow—
one
faltering
step
of
mankind
after
another
through this deepening gloom,
in winter
the graves overflow.

THE EMPORER'S NEW CLOTHES

Aging,
This President stands before us looking
Youthful and vigorous
And speaks in honeyed phrases that soothe
And reassure,
The old deceptions heard in every age—
Of greed and disregard—
To ears to eager to believe; not even
A child to warn them
That like all the others before, these
Are not new clothes—
Merely another naked emperor.

GIVE ME IRON MEN

Give me iron men and iron mountains
The poet's plea—
They have always imagined it so—
And history has answered
With men who have made a difference
Both good and evil, yet
Always with manageable consequence;
These new tools will change that
And we shall not think them
Iron men, but pitiful, dying
With the rest, whining and sniveling
In floods of excrement from loosened bowels.

ONE SPRING MORE

So much to say
        so little time
                so many ways
To say it
        how is it no one
                wants to hear
These sounds
        leaves cascading silently
                under autumn's pressing burden
Minstrels of the season
        on every path abound
                faces turned to rain-soaked
Trunks
        gray flannel oaks
                softly dripping promise
Yet another spring
        and another
                and another
Till it ends
        for each of us
                and then for all
If ever
        can it really matter when
                or how
These stones
        cold smooth dumb
                and frozen lumps

Of clay
        forever swirling round
                a world
Neither void
        nor matter
                but both
And mindless mystery besides
        if then
                why not now
Birds
        flowers
                if viewed
Too closely
        mirror this mystery
                and everything falls apart
we must believe it
        already we treat it
                so
just one more spring
        we hope
                and follow winter's progress
Yet will not hear
        the warnings
                clearer than these
Damp earth
        and rocks
                thrust aside

By the budding crocus
        soft warm winds
                sigh
The sounds
        of our relief
                this one spring more.

ROWAN OAK

Rowan Oak stands empty—silent
Like its master—
Veiled in gray despair of deepening December dusk
        and
The verdant decadence of untended cedar
And magnolia—
A haunting melancholy stares from its darkened
        windows
Like his sorrowful eyes
That moved the playwright to tears.

Mostly neglected—
Like he was in his lifetime
There are still those here who would like to
        forget
Few have read even one of the books
He gave his life to
Or ever paused to wonder why it mattered—
Honored and acclaimed he had by then
Poured out his soul too often
And the scars ran deep

A poet he called himself—
Not for the failed volumes of poetry
But a spiritual kinship with
Homer and Aeschylus and Euripides
A writer's writer—they knew

So much talent, warned Sherwood Anderson,
        if you aren't
Careful you won't write anything
Hemingway for his short stories, said
        Steinbeck, but
Faulkner for anything he ever wrote—
The best we have had—
He wrote with his heart on his sleeve
Such consuming passion only genius could
        sustain—
"A life's work in the agony and sweat of the
Human spirit," he would say in Stockholm,
"About the human heart in conflict with
Itself which alone can make good writing
Because only that is worth writing about,
Worth the agony and the sweat"—
And they knew

He became this place—
Jefferson and Yoknapatawpha County along the
Tallahatchie River—
Compson's Mile, Sutpen's Hundred
The Big Woods
Waystops on a chart of the imagination,
His own little postage stamp of native soil
        so rich
He could never live long enough to exhaust it
And didn't—
In the years since

Faulkner country has changed
And is changeless
Having passed to the trust of others who will
Make of it what they will
But can never erase the words
By which he made it his

Now a generation has passed—
Another generation lived in the constant
        realization
We could all be blown up
And the words take on new significance—"I
Decline to accept the end of man," he had said,
"I believe that man will not merely endure:
He will prevail."
And in that, the poet's last wish
And greatest promise—
Such men peer deeply, passionately
And we may hope with clearer vision
Though others would disagree;
Behind the veil of gray despair that dusk has drawn
This place is strangely silent
And empty
The words but fading echoes in the stillness
As I strain to hear the poet's last wish
And turn again
Toward one spring more.

From *Journal Entries*

SEATTLE, SEPT '86

Through the cobbled streets
up a hill from
Pike Place Market, past
alcoves along the
alley, there
scrawled on the wall
in the blaring spray-paint
sounds of silence:

Poetry Lives—

The city blinks and
whispers its answer,
in the bustle and noise of crowds,
the distant scream
of sirens...

8/86

Searing,
As though on hot pavement,
Spilling your guts
At their feet
For all the world to see,
Flinching—
Not from pain
But fear,
That someone will know
It is your guts,
Or worse—
That they won't.

IF AT ALL

It isn't simple.
It is all very complicated. Nothing
ever changes that, no degree of understanding
or sophistication, the green hills and
barren deserts by which we stumbled our way
here bleeding and unabsolved, burdened
with images: recalled later they explain
nothing, fit no algorithm, give rise to
no principle, and can only be expressed
in words unredeeming; we
store them up one by one then struggle
to write these lines that some one or two
may say what was meant, uncertain
what it is, or if anyone can ever
know. Nothing ever changes that—
no amount of time or reason,
no experience or wisdom: whatever
we know, we know unknowingly,
if at all.

A PARABLE

A single voice and new,
Coaxed halting from the shadows
Of its solitude, and sounding
Still its desolation, drew
From all those others
That had gone before
In ways it never knew,
And never could restore.

THE UNAESTHETIC TRUTH

Like all things real they were
Flawed, here and there ink stains
On the pages that I bartered
For their praise and money. Later,
When the harsh words had smitten,
They cursed me for my candor
And charged me with dishonesty,
Pointing to the unaesthetic truth.

PALTRY WAGES

One verse
Then two
The first one pink
The next one blue,
Then joy is streaked
By tears in time
The cadence clumsy
Strained the rhyme,
As sorrow yields
To grief and worse
The stanzas lengthen
Verse by verse,
Till what is earned
Is truth itself—
A stingy, biting
Penurious wealth.

5/25/86

Days and nights of endless striving—
All this
And more will still be here
Long after I am gone—
Growing older is but to grasp
That one essential truth;
Why then confront inexhaustible folly
With words
And such a puny fury?
Because we shall not be here
And must have the answer sooner.

THE NATURAL HISTORIAN
(To R. S.)

A twinkle in the eye
Conceals a mind
Too flinty
For such soft deception;
The bees dance to a tune
Unknown, Arachne's
Tapestry tells no truths,
Merely observe—
The intricate steps, each
Silken strand—
No answers, but questions
Their patterns reveal,
Save one:
This the only truth.

REQUIEM

These Greeks turned it back upon
    itself,
Made the gods too mortal and
    killed them:
Anthropomorphic death—
Replacing them instead with this
    stingy materialism
From which we have yet to recover,
Bent upon following their reason
    lean and hungry
Like a wolf on the slopes of Mt. Ida
To wherever its prey seeks refuge.
They were right you know—
    only
Man cannot live this way.

THE CONVOY

Distinct
against the autumn
haze it crawls
segmented
like a many-legged
dragon through the
riotous countryside,
the feet Europe
the serpentine head
Vietnam
the great camouflaged body
Grenada
Managua
or Havana—
here where there
is no war,
where there is only
the fading warmth
of the equinox
and the first faint promise
of winter,
the creatures of war
crawl about
and make ready.

"FORTH" OF JULY

O lofty Pericles, gifted orator
Where art thou
At the hour of our greatest need
Who spoke
In polished phrases like gleaming marble
The golden lies
That made men yet awhile
Want to strive
And sacrifice for Athens. These modern lies
They speak
Like rough-hewn stone are only base
And foolish
From which to cringe in shame,
Yet serve
As well for these Athenians. Your
Flowery speech
Was wasted Pericles, less noble words
Will do—
The result, I fear, the same.

WILLIAM CARLOS WILLIAMS

The awkward
little poems
he wrote
in strangely
broken lines
kept running
broken through
my thoughts
to suddenly
join together
un broken
just the
way he
had intended.

EXPECT SMALL DIFFERENCES

The great evils—
Those worthy of this shining we call civilization—
Are with us always:
Straining and labor of the masses
And the people speak, the deed done, some new foulness
Revealed—we recoil in horror,
But mostly later. In this we show ourselves overmatched,
The prescience of the mind outdone by the individual strivings
Of so many bits of sentience all laboring together
Or at cross purposes—we do not know beforehand:
Those crematoria which belched the pall of smoke
And stench of death across a ravaged Europe
Somehow no worse than the gentle fall of raindrops
Laced with acids
To leach away the stain. Hitler again in time
Will have his supporters, Caligula is but an abstraction
Across so many centuries: distance and time cleanse
Everything the same, and who knows
How the future will unfold?
Sometimes it seems that it is either all good, or all evil,
These two great faces we cannot tell apart. In that
There is no solace to deny these words, this torment—
Yet from far enough away it will seem so:

The choking city-haze, the crimson-tinctured sunsets
Will wear both countenances,
The blinding plutonium flash
Signal the start of some new epoch. Caution then,
And calm; treat them both the same: they are twins
Good and evil. Speak of them often
And in the same breath, the same measured tones—
Each equally deserving. Where there is such perfection
Expect small differences.

THE DELTA

i)

gray
December
days,
dripping
and bitter cold,
the damp chill
heavy—
with the sweat of slaves
the old Negro told me:
the Delta.

ii)

This land lies buried fallow
beneath
a lifetime of memories,
deeper
than the rich black soil,
richer
and more fallow still.

iii)

To be young
and innocent
in a troubled toil-worn land,

fresh footprints
stamped in the soft soil—
the land wears a new smile
to ward off the old sorrow.

iv)

I crawled up on his lap—
The memory I have
is of the smell of the old Negro,
soft and musty
like soiled cotton flannel,
and of the graying nap on his head—
I ran my youthful hands over it—
You gotta make sump'm o' yo'self
he would tell me,
the tobacco-stained teeth showing through
his smile,
But the cloudy distant eyes held a vacant
faraway look
that told another story.

v)

His old shack burned down one night—
It sat across the street
behind the church—
She saved his life,
they said,
beating on the door to wake him
A pot of water on the stove boiled dry
and melted
He was almost blind.
I never saw him much again after that

He finally got too old
I guess—
I never even thought about him being black,
until later,
or ever did find out
if it mattered to him that I was not.

vi)

Sitting cocked on his head the most
unlikely felt fedora with
one hand

he would lift it up scratch the balding
nap with long bony fingers then wipe
his brow and replace it all in one

easy motion the
smooth black face
solemn

framed by a stiff white collar and
sloping shoulders and the tan
gabardine windbreaker

he wore summer and winter un-zippered
at the neck to
reveal a shiny threadbare

tie
fastened at the waist around
the tops of trousers that

reached to shoes too
long unpolished ever
to be again he

looked the part no
ordinary field hand
but

the foreman the only
one who could
bridge

this graying
gap
between black and white.

vii)

The face was stern it
had to be
that way but the eyes

compassionate he could say
yessuh without ever revealing
himself the way

he had done
for forty years or more
then relay

the orders on down the
line without being
harsh yet still

stern which was why
he was the
black boss the master's

nigger though the others
never held it against
him he managed

to live just a little
better
because of it.

viii)

I love this land
Why? Does
one need

a reason beyond the fact?
besides
I grew up here

I understand its seasons
and
its many moods

its injustices
and hatreds
and bigotry

its tortured cry
of anguish
the dark stains of its past

yet I love it
just the same
can

there be
any
other reason?

ix)

I love this land
Somewhere
in the distance

without ever having
to explain
why

a cottonwood
quakes
beneath it

a wild boar
its spine
pierced

with an arrow
three
young savages

kneel
around their
trophy

MOUNDS

Each
starts out a
sensation some

idea or
mental image a
bump

on the memory around
which words
are piled

neatly
for the most part
but easily

jumbled if you aren't
too careful
smoothed and

patted into place
who knows
at the outset

which
will make a neat
mound?

MORAL

A field of daisies
is a fitting subject
for a poem white-petaled

they twist on slender
stalks in unison
to peer

yellow-eyed
at the sun's progress that
alone

is more than adequate
reason or stand head
bowed

in prayerful posture throughout
the night oh and
what about the

occasional maverick
did I mention
in unison who

doesn't follow the
crowd isn't there
a moral

there where so much
is possible little
is accomplished.

C. PISSARRO, 1866

It is a large canvas
a dirt road
along the banks of the Marne

in winter
focuses one's attention to sweep
from the lower left

to the upper right there
the sky lighter
we finally escape the

dark feeling
of the canvas as a whole
and instead

become engulfed in its
luminous tones a woman and
her child

walk the road beside
leafless trees
swallowed up

by the depths of its
richness it is
quite simply

that unmistakable thing
a masterpiece there
are few colors mostly

greens
and grays
and fewer shapes yet

with them the artist
has created a
universe this

is not properly the beginning of
something new
but the

triumph
of all that
is timeless.

MANET'S BAR AT THE FOLLIES-BERGERE

Here facing us
is a young woman her
back

to a mirror the
artist
has taken liberties

with the reflections art
he believed
obeys its own rules yet

we must clearly understand
that it is a
mirror

life
has a depth not
evident

in the flat figure of the young woman
her eyes
vacant

but not unexpressive stare
fixed
straight ahead

masking
what is in her thoughts
for that

we must look much
deeper
in the mirror behind.

IMPRESSIONISM

Shadows
have color
whether

Monet or
Pissarro realized it
first

or even Renoir
does not concern us
now it might

almost be taken
as the abstract aesthetic
of impressionism

art
not how we react
to the little

incidents
of our daily lives
though

it would certainly
be appropriate
there too.

A LIGHTED CANDLE

She lights a candle
where no candle is needed
in the several-hundred-watt glare

of the room
which its flame cannot pierce
but its incense can

a candle
whose virtue
is its very superfluousness

registered in a flickering symbolism;
Pasternak
—said Yevteshenko—

was a candle of conscience
not a beacon
the way a small flame

is more noticeable
for not dispelling entirely
what gives it form;

this one it seems
is to signal
some small protest

of her own
of modernity itself perhaps
of the several-hundred-watt glare

and the global combustion
that lights it too harshly
dispelling

every shadowed sanctuary
how to escape it
in this day

except
in the simple gesture
of a lighted candle;

there is a power
in such small symbols
what is whispered

is often more significant
than a thousand shouts;
better to light a single candle

that way to admire
the dancing flame
and acknowledge the darkness too.

MONTANA MONSTER

Pivoted by its tail
it writhes
in great circles

upon the ground
metal spine and truss-work
ribs

held high
on tubular legs rubber-
footed stretch

segmented
across the field
preying-mantis-like

its transparent body of
soft mist glistening
in the sun

anoints with life-
giving elixir all
it touches

here the last great
monsters left their
bones

and footprints fossilized
in dry creek beds
and barren

rock who
will find the footprints
and skeletons

of these monsters
or know
what created them?

SELF PORTRAIT: VAN GOGH

The face goes through a metamorphosis
Canvas after canvas—there are
In all about forty of them, this
One of the last is likewise the best—
As does the palette of colors
And the life itself, the artist
Intent upon confronting his own image:
The piercing eyes stare more intensely, the face
Ever more haggard, charged with emotion;
The red beard casts a gangrenous pall
Over the sallow skin, the colors brighter, more
Shimmering project a feeling of madness apparent
In the features and in the events of his life;
The severed ear is not visible though the impulse
Wielding the shears is evident enough.
Gauguin could not help but be impressed:
The background swirls and dances magically
On the canvas, ominously, as if events
Had gotten out of hand, to feel the soft
Bristles in the sticky oils as the colors
On the rough cloth take shape—this
No commercial art, but the creation of a man
Obsessed with capturing at that instant
In one space all that he had lived for;
Gauguin the charlatan was indeed impressed:
He had looked into the very face of art.

A CHANGE OF MOOD

The gray beneath the firs
outside my window

the lighter gray (but not
white) of the paper

the gray
familiar marks across the page

have all smothered
with their grayness

the sunshine
by which I had hoped to write.

AIDS, 7/89

I.

In the first instance
there was of course
free love or at least
unfettered (they are
wrong about that) there
being then no cures
but no microbes either

Vengeance is mine
saith the Lord but
European arrogance was
more effective—it was contact
with the New World
that rotted Gauguin's brain

except for where
as now
reason or belief could
constrain erect passions—
about that
there was never any mistaking

then finally there were medicines
(though they had been there

in the bread mold
all along) and no one
had of necessity
to perish though some
still did and do

but now passion prevails
as of course
it always has and
not reason or belief
(there being no cures)
can forestall the
biological conclusion.

II.

The object has always been

to get as many seeds
into the bellies of as many women

as necessary
to procreate the race

there has always been
some price to pay

those who see it as something else
think only in terms

of possibilities
never getting beyond

that fateful deception
who is to say

that where what is possible
conflicts with necessity

there are any possibilities?

POETRY SUITS ME FINE

Being a poet suits me fine.
Mystery is it, certainty's a gag
We play on ourselves and one
Arm twisted up behind your back.
Let the philosophers hunt in circles
Let the scientists search for truth.
What can be explained is not poetry,
Said Yeats, and that's all right by me.
Being a poet suits me fine.

THE PEOPLE KNEW

They are not to be trusted, the leaders on both sides told
                the people.
See the destruction of two wars, the death of millions,
                the fields of gleaming gravestones.
And one side: See the ghettos and the slums, the poverty
                and the prejudice.
And the other: See the loss of freedom, the abuse of human rights.
And both: Their people are enslaved still, and their leaders would
                conquer the world. We must be strong, arm ourselves,
                prepare to annihilate the other side.

Now the walls are coming down, the barriers are being dismantled
Brick by brick. The historians, the political scientists, the thinkers,
They do not know why, they did not predict it.
They were all caught unawares.

The people knew.
They told the politicians, the world leaders
On both sides, enough is enough. You are wrong.
We are tired of your way, your arguments make no sense.
You are merely foolish, said the people, we will not follow you.

The leaders were wrong. They thought only of themselves.
They listened to their own arguments and heard only what
They wanted to hear, believed only what they wanted
To believe. The leaders were not to be trusted.
The people knew.

WHY IS THAT?

Some people hold an idea more real than an acorn.
Why is that?
Out of one can grow a tree, a forest, and a wilderness
                stretching endlessly from sunrise to sunset;
Out of the other can grow an action that levels the forest,
                and raises up in its place farms and settlements
                and great cities and civilizations, and books and music
                and works of art, and the sort of determination
                that men are willing to die for.
Why is that?
One can provide food and shelter and fires for warmth;
The other fuels the fires that make food and shelter
                and warmth not enough.
Why is that?

WRITTEN IN STONE

I love you Patti—
He wrote it high up on the hillside
In stones laid out in long straight rows
Big enough for all to see as they rode
Back and forth to town or went about
Their chores. The stones gleamed white
In the summer sun. In winter
They glistened in the rain and mist.
The cows ate the grass around them
And the woodchucks left them undisturbed.
Years later, they could still be seen,
Long after he had changed his mind.

THE SAILBOATS

The sailboats teeter in the wind
They thrust their arms upward
And cup their hands and hold them out to catch the breeze.
Their hulls, hissing, slice through the waves.

The sailboats scurry and weave before the wind
Their sails billow in the breezes
Little rows of silvery bubbles spread out behind.
The hulls make a thin smile
And bow and nod to the waves.

ROBERT SERVICE

When I read this simple verse of his
My head goes round and round
As in and out march images
To a cadence of measured sounds,
In a few tight lines he tells a story
Tells it straight and true
Of how he cremated Sam McGee
Or the death of Dan McGrew,
Of nights alone and books unread
And things for which he had no time
So that he might toil instead
To capture thoughts in verse and rhyme,
That I might sit and sip my sherry
And in one or two such lines
Find some truth for the worn and weary
To repay him for his time.

SEASIDE DAWN

This thin, lone cry
traveling down the dwindling night
will usher in a dawn
still and dripping,
the shrouded sun
wrapped in fog, and
muted promise of what
for the several seasons
allotted no one
I have spent the hours
shirking, till now
the smooth, worn tires
on the wet sand
leave tracks more distinct:
the patient water
seeps back in and
washes them away again;
though, for all that,
the beach years later
is not the same.

From *Neither Here Nor There*

Thomas Grissom

NEITHER HERE
NOR THERE

Poems

ORDER OUT OF CHAOS

The witless winds of wisdom scour the land
And pile debris haphazard in old fence corners:

Turn not your back on the disorder of the world
Printed on the pages of discarded newspapers

Shun not the delicate details of detritus
Marooned in abandoned mounds of middens;

Plastered to the earth in rain-soaked sheets
Long forgotten news may yet make sense

Heaped in some remote out of the way place
Even a pile of junk may have left some trace.

TROUT ARE PHILOSOPHERS

A single line
written
on a scrap of paper hastily

abbreviated
by a momentary but fleeting clarity
one

of many thoughts that come
and go
like fish trailing flies

the world spinning
on beyond the meaning
long ago

forgotten
trout are philosophers
it said

then
and still does now
though

neither they
nor I
nor the spinning world know why.

POEMS BY—

I like the style, his technique—
No, really; I do—
The clever cryptic choice of words
The sudden surprising twist and turn,
The unanticipated image—trouble is,
I don't know what the hell he is saying
Half the time—then what is there
To like? It is poetry isn't it,
Or merely one more empty riddle
To nothing new under the sun?
I don't want my poetry
To be something I have to study—
Damn it man, could it be the fault
Is not entirely mine?

THE BEST OF JOHN PRINE

There we were at the Tacoma Dome
With maybe twenty thousand other folks
All jammed too close together, into cheap plastic seats—
Mostly facing the wrong way,
Too far back to see—

And the loud speaker—
Reminding you that drinking is permitted
Only in the lounge
And smoking's not allowed,
And they probably don't want you to fart, either

And up there on the stage
Ol' John Prine
Singing "Angel from Montgomery"
And "It's a Big Old Goofy World"—
Sippin' on a drink between songs,
Smoking a cigarette,
And probably farting too, if he got the urge.

WILLIAM TELL

I placed on his youthful head, trusting,
Even eager, whose face across the empty years
I can no longer recall beyond the vaguest notion
And yet the most specific recollection

The empty cardboard box—cylindrical, tall,
With its figure of a smiling Quaker
Whose broad beaming countenance
Replaces in the dark light of memory
His own forgotten face,
But whose pacific smile could not shield
Against the sure swift flight
Of my arrow

And plotted my purpose:
To lay at his feet
In the burning sun and choking dust
That empty box impaled upon my shaft,
The deed likewise impaled forever in fame
And spirit, soaring and yearning
By that one act of youthful daring
To finally escape that place;
Then stepped off one pace for each
Of the fingers on those two hands
That would do the deed

And drew the bow,
Its graceful limbs bent
Like the crescent of a new moon
Replacing now that blinding sun
In my dream haunted sleep,
Recalling his eyes
Held tightly closed
The way I had instructed
That he might not move and spoil the shot

Or worse. And feeling
The linen cord cutting deeply
Across the three last digits,
And taut muscles holding back the strong string,
Aimed at the static smiling face
Six inches above that pale flat space
Between his closed eyes

And shot.
The shaft a blurred streak of light
Glistening in the sun
Stood Zeno-like in that intervening space
And hummed its indifferent song
The air vibrant with the danger
Of its choice, yet
Unerringly seeking out the pacific countenance
To spare that other faceless one
And keep my hopes,

And his, alive.
The dust in little puffs spurted
As the fallen box and smiling face
Danced, squirming, on its feathered axis
About that plain bare space between us,
As it does still
In my dream disturbed slumbers

Then came to rest.
And he willing, even eager,
To face again the flying shaft
And see this time
The deed done that I would never do,
Could never do again,
Who, in spirit soaring and yearning
To finally escape that place
Gambled all on that one shot

And lost. Held fast
By that other nameless one
Whose face across the empty years
I can no longer recall beyond the vaguest notion
And yet the most specific recollection,
Impaled like that broad smiling countenance
Lying motionless in the dust,
Bound forever in deed and memory
To that never forgotten place.

MIDNIGHT SUN

We met above the Arctic Circle, in
Inuvik, Northwest Territories, no
Road farther north. We had something in common:
He was a German, without prejudices
He said, from Dortmund, and knew the elder Von Braun;
I was a physicist up from the South,
Also without prejudices, I told him,
And knew the son. Once a roofer, he liked
To say he looked down on people, and owned
A hotel and a place in Edmonton
Another one in Acapulco. He
Enjoyed talking with physicists, he said,
Especially one who knew a student of Sommerfeld's
And so we passed the time. He talked freely
About himself, I listened to his story.
A Hitler Youth, mining in the Cassiar Range,
Mushrooms in Edmonton, and now this, the finest
Hotel in the Arctic, a millionaire twice over
And self-made, with all the usual complaints
About how things are now. He showed me the three
Bars, the grand ballroom, he had built it all
With his own hands. Three floors completed and two
More planned when the beautiful Brunhilde
(That is what he called her) had ordered him
To stop. "She is so beautiful," he told me with
A twinkle in his steel gray eyes, "but oh,
So brutal. What brings you to the North?"
"Wilderness," I answered, "and because I have never

Seen it." "Wilderness," he scoffed. "Then say for
The sake of space and solitude," I offered instead.
He was not easily put off, "I have had
Too much of space and solitude for one life,"
He said. "Solitude is merely something you think
You want only when you don't have it. Men
Were not meant to be alone but together.
This hotel full of people is all the solitude
I want," he said, "and what good is all that space
When there's nothing here to put in it? Ah,
But for my part, I wish I could sell the frigging
Place and get the hell out," he confessed.
I might have accused him that he had both—
Yet seemed to want neither, but it
Would not have been an act of kindness
Befitting his place as host. Afterwards
I made my way back to my camp and my tent,
He to catch a plane to Edmonton.
We each had come our different ways to be here,
I thought, and had something more in common.
The sun wouldn't set at all that night, but from our
Different directions the world was closing in on us.

AUGURY

There are dark forces about
O Lords and Ladies
They walk the wide earth with impunity
And reach to the very bounds of heaven
And can be seen long afterwards
In a severed chicken's neck.

WHAT

What is there to write?
That the earth is not flat
But round
And the sun neither sets nor rises
But the shining earth, swimming in its light,
Turns steadily toward it?

This is no longer the new world—
Nor yet the old—
And can never again be either.

Facts, once confronted
Soon run their course, give way
To thoughts, and we are left
With that which has never been written:
The mystery behind the facts—
I only began to live my life
When I knew it was going to end.

FALSE STARTS

—"You don't sound like a scientist,"
he said to me—
"Good," I thought.

On the desk
Ehrenfeld's
The Arrogance of Humanism:
In it the bookmark—
A lottery ticket.

Nothing now is left
Of the tiny thicket beside the house,
Except my too long story
About the woman and the fawn
And the solitary inscrutable old dog.

JEFFERS REDUX

That the age will decline, civilizations crumble, and man turn murderous
Is true enough, but mostly irrelevant. That hawk and rock and windswept wave
Are symbols of the natural beauty of things is true also, but a truth that bestows
No salvation. These truths are powerless against the necessity of life, impotent
Against the need for man to act. Not mountains nor desert nor the trans-human
       beauty,
But man, is the measure of things: Lacking man's consciousness—the inward eye
Turned outward—the universe is but mindless matter, devoid of beauty or meaning.
That things are beautiful we do not need great poets to tell us: beauty is printed
       plainly
On each man's soul. That man deceives and betrays and is frequently deluded
Is nothing new. Yet hunger and desire and the need for shelter have created great
       civilizations;
Curiosity and insatiable craving for answers, great discoveries; passion and yearning,
Great music, art, and poetry. These too are beautiful: man is part of the beauty.
These things we do not need great poets to tell us: Not *how*
But *why*: the vast unquenchable mystery of why.

ALL IS MYSTERY

These things we know:
That the universe is expanding
That it has been for a long time
That it may continue to expand forever,
That stars form galaxies and galaxies clusters and they in turn
Clusters of clusters on a scale unimaginable,
That the elements are formed from hydrogen and helium in the furnace of the
       stars
Spewed throughout the cosmos by the cataclysmic crescendo of a star's death
       throes,
That something earlier gave rise to hydrogen and helium,
That we who know these things are made from this same stardust—
But know little else besides,
Not what came before nor what will come afterward—
All but these few things are uncertain and shrouded in mystery.
The Pythagoreans believed all was number, Empedocles that love and strife
Brought all into being from earth, air, fire, and water; Leucippus thought
All was made of atoms and the void, for Plato it was the elusive Forms: for us
Electrons, photons, and quarks, and this too is surely doomed to failure;
For Heraclitus was right: Nature loves to hide, and the oracle
At Delphi neither speaks nor conceals, but gives signs: All is mystery.

THE COSMOLOGICAL PRINCIPLE

Everywhere and in every direction
The same, except here
On this blue and white speck:
It required Copernicus, Kepler, Galileo, and Newton
To convince us that Aristotle and Ptolemy were wrong—
A legion of thinkers since
Have only deepened the mystery—
Wispy strands of matter swirl, compress, catch fire
And explode spewing stardust through the void and
We are the result: nowhere the same
Everywhere different, there is nothing else like us:
The mystery deepens, no cosmological principle
Can mask our difference amid the vastness
Of all this sameness, not Darwin surely
Or even a few strands of DNA, they are no better
Really than the older stories—
We just are, the beginning and the end,
Born of and returning to
The mystery.

THE VAST UNQUENCHABLE MYSTERY

That there is no Christian God—how could there be?—scarcely needs saying,
No Islamic God or Hebrew God: none of the little narrow-eyed, human-hating
        gods—
Only the one undeniable God: the vast unquenchable mystery at the core of
        things.
Out of the mystery we emerged, and to it we return; between birth and death
        we harbor it
In our hearts, nurturing and worshipping it; or fearing and denying it
Seek solace in the countenance of these other grinning, gap-toothed gods.
It will not be denied. The mystery is beautiful but also terrible. Science
Disguises it in the tawdry cloak of description, answering *how* but never *why*
And, lately, even that scant little more sparingly. Our minds have played a trick
On us. With them we have probed the vast cosmos and the tiniest microcosm
Discovering at the heart of each the mystery our minds cannot know—
Reason stymied by itself. If there is *any* mystery, it is *all* mystery
And our questions all unanswerable, and that is both beautiful and terrible—
The choice is ours. Choose the God of mystery:
That way to make the beauty less terrible.

UNSIMPLE LIES

I have had too much of God—and gods—
Invoked where they are powerless and impotent:
To explain what is unexplainable—
Or intruding where they are least welcome
And most harmful: to hide behind and alibi
What only humans can decide—though I confess
I much prefer the latter to the former: gods
To God—if any god is needed, surely
All are; the mystery of this world so far
Exceeds the bounds of any single God,
Or even a host of deities, we may as well
For all that heed Lucretius and dispense
With them completely for atoms and the void,
And rid ourselves of fear and superstition:
If by God we mean we cannot understand,
Leave it at that—more honest than to turn
That simple truth into such unsimple lies.

THE ANCIENT QUARREL

Poetry is a sleight of hand—turning
One thing obscure into another clear—
Plato knew it, and early became the Master
Poet—when logic fails fall back upon
Metaphor and the power of language to persuade—
He most often did, and we love him for it.
Language is lovelier by far than logic
And more convincing too, the nature of the world
Makes certainty a gag while granting the existence
Of possibilities, the very art of poetry—
That's what the Poet in Plato understood:
Plato's arguments are fatally flawed
Any beginner can spot the errors—
The irony of Socrates to point them out—
But his instincts were true and pure
And we grant him the benefit of the doubt
Seduced by the sweetness of his rhetoric.
Plato the Philosopher quarreled with the Poets
Accusing them of lying about the gods
And banished them from the Republic—
The Poets—the Poets lie too much, mocked Nietzsche—
No, not lies, Plato, but a skillful sleight of hand
Turning one thing obscure into another clear:
The hard unavoidable truths—lacking which
Philosophy, Plato, is but a gilded web of deception.

CONFESSION

If by God you mean
Nature and the physical universe—
I am the most devout of acolytes;
If by it you mean anything beyond the mystery
And wonder of the present moment—
I am the most doubting of atheists.

SYMMETRY

There is a poetry of sadness, and a poetry of solace
And they are not different they are the same
The same song speaks both, and the same words—
The going away is but the coming again, and
Whatever is lost is what is gained. Along with these,
Also a third, a poetry of solitude and silence
And it too is not different, it too is the same—
In the solitude of sadness, the solace of silence—
In the silence of sadness, the solace of solitude:
In the silence of solitude and the solitude of silence
The refrains of sadness and solace sound the same.

THE BACCAE

It is a decided
defect
of the modern world

that
the quality of magic
is missing

It is for this
that we are seduced
by

tragedy
and believe
in evil.

THE SUFFERER AND THE SECRET CAUSE

Did he ever read the words on the page
And wonder how on earth they came to be,
How from that diminutive boy whose laughter
He heard chase childhood into youth,
Turned suddenly quiet and serious,
Could erupt in bursts so unrestrained
Such depth of passion
Page after accumulating page,
Or was he by then too defeated
To even wonder—

Whether he had perhaps left too soon
While there was still some chance at redemption—
His if not the tormented young man's—
But cast away in the anger
And shame of failure
To leave him with only the agonizing questions
And amazement
At the mounting words on the pages
That by then had grown too numerous
To deny,
Staring back at him,
Contemptuously mocking his error—

And the young man—
Did the torrent of words make the loss more bearable
And sooth the hurt and rejection,
Or did they further divide and separate

And become in the silent depths of night
A bitter victory—

Did the long passage of time
Bring them peace and reconciliation,
Or merely deepen by its growing silence
The gulf between them
Until neither could fathom any way
To cross its treacherous depths—

Did the words on the printed pages
By which so many hearts have been united
With the sufferer and the secret cause
Become in turn the secret cause
That made sufferers of them both?

DEVOTION

It must have been hard on her, possessing
Neither the kind of willful disregard nor the freedom of spirit
To throw off the prejudices of her day, lying there instead
Quietly in the dark while he groped and then
Found her through the many passionless nights
And the three children, waiting patiently for him
To finish and fall back because it was her duty—
Agreed to in the union of marriage but also out of
Feeling and genuine affection for him, unable to summon
The same dark desire or reckless abandon though
Awestruck and a little afraid of his, until finally
It ended in separate beds and then in separate rooms—
She relieved that it was at last over, he resigned
By then to let the embers of his youth cool and extinguish—
As though what they had become bore
No relation to what they once had been:
Let no one pity them the pleasures missed, the lost
Opportunity, not every star burns as brightly and all
Are cold and silent in that fathomless blackness:
Devotion was flame and heat intense enough for them.

SACRED POEMS AND PRIVATE EJACULATIONS

Her desiccated juices
crusted thin
upon the pendulous dangle

flakes and scales
at my coaxing grasp
to rain

upon the fallow floor
the detritus
of desire deprived

like the dandruff
of some itch
unscratched

why should we not
take things in hand
and write

in jetted streams
of alabaster
a more fitting finish?

CONFIRMATION

A voice mocked: "God is dead."
"Liar, blasphemer," the People cried—
But that was all.
None, though they tried,
Could accost the speaker,
For none could determine from whence the voice.
Only "Liar, blasphemer," they clamored loudly—
And by their urgent cry of protest confirmed
What the secret scornful voice affirmed.

SUCH SACRILEGE

God bless America? Perhaps. But why?
One hundred fifty years ago we were a nation
Of slaveholders, keeping an entire race of people
In bondage and chattel slavery. A nation divided
We fought a bloody and murderous war to resolve the issue
But didn't. For the next one hundred years both sides alike
Schemed and tricked and dissembled, and looked the other way
To deny justice and social equality to former slaves, freed
But never free. Nor was it that different for Asians and others of color
And those of religious and social distinctions: Native Americans,
Chinese, Japanese, Irish and Italians, Catholics and Protestants,
Hispanics, Latinos, Jews and Muslims, women and gays—the list has
    been writ
Many ways. God bless America? Perhaps. Yet evidently
Not all are blessed equally. One nation under God?
Such nonsense. Such rubbish and hypocrisy.

BEING AND NOTHINGNESS

Why is there anything at all? And if
Something, why *this* something and not *some other*?
Is it because, as the Eleatics believed,
There cannot be *nothing*; that Nothingness
Is only an illusion suggested by Being,
The way unicorns are suggested by horses?
But that does not explain *this* something. The only conclusion
Is that, if anything at all, then everything imaginable,
And our attempts to understand it are as futile
And unending as the endless variety conceivable,
And perhaps sometime, somewhere unicorns do exist.
Perhaps there is no all encompassing universe,
But a multi-verse of many parallel universes,
Each different in some respect from all the others
And language fails and must be expanded.
This idea by physicists was conceived to conceal
A profound embarrassment: the failure to reconcile
Quantum theory with cosmology, the extreme
Antipodes of our understanding; the one describing
A discrete microcosm of discontinuities, the other
A continuous cosmic mesh of smoothness. But it is not
Science, nevertheless, for no one can ever know—
What a theory allows is nowise demanded—
Merely a cunning conjecture by clever Poets
Dreaming idly of unicorns.

EPISTEMOS

Science in the twentieth century has reshaped our view of the world
But mostly wrongly:
Not the oracle of certainty as was believed in the nineteenth century
But Prometheus bound
Chained and nailed to his rock, limited, his ambitions thwarted. Each
Advance in understanding paid for by an intrinsic limitation
In our ultimate knowledge of the world. Relativity imposes
The finite velocity of light as the limiting speed of our experience
Relegating knowledge always to the past. Quantum theory restricts
Determinism in the realm of the microcosm. Cosmology reveals
An ever-expanding universe accelerating toward complete emptiness.
Chaos theory describes a non-linear world deterministic
Yet inherently unpredictable. And like Prometheus
We find ourselves bound by chains forged from the links
Of our own cleverness
In uncovering the secrets of the universe. Only biology remains
A completely deterministic science, and only because it has yet
To discover its own ultimate truth.
Why did we think it otherwise? What the gods give they also
Take away.

HALLELUJAH CHORUS

I can get along without this
Hey, yes I can
I can get along without this
O Lord, yes I can
I was doing so before now
I can do so once again
They'll never notice I'm not here
Never know that I am gone
By the time they finally miss me
I'll be singing a whole new song
They'll never even remember me
Never recall that I was here
By the time they think of me again
It'll be this time next year
By then I'll be gone so far
Be gone so far away
Wherever it is I end up
It'll be a brand new day
I'll find myself so busy
New friends and loves and such
Whatever I have to leave behind
Won't matter all that much
I can get along without this
Hey, yes I can
I can get along without this
O Lord, yes I can.

CURVED SPACE

I'm not thinking right
Or maybe I am
It's coming down hard
It may be a slam
Some things seem right
And some things are not
But I can't tell which
And I mostly forgot
The world lines do this
The world lines do that
And the space is all curved
The space is too fat
And one place is when
And another is where
The first one is here
The other one there
The beginning is the end
The bottom is the top
And the arrow of time
Doesn't start or stop
It doesn't come full circle
Or swing back again
You never can return
Where you've already been
And maybe I knew it

It's just hard to say
With the sun still shining
On a drab, dreary day
And some things are right
And some things are not
And I can't tell which
And I mostly forgot.

FOR WHOM

The terrible toning of the bells
The dreary, dirgeful droning of the bells
The distant, mournful moaning of the bells
The ceaseless, grinding groaning of the bells;
And all the world is called to conclave
And all the world pauses to tell
For whom the terrible tolling of the bells.

CAMUS

Just because everything is permitted
Does not mean nothing is forbidden.

In a world where
The only certainty
Is death—
And the benign indifference of the
Universe to man—
Anything is possible
Even murder,
And nothing is important
Not even life—
And the only path to happiness
Is an utter lack
Of hope.

SELF-EVALUATION

I have trained the young people well—
Those eager few who have been receptive—they go on
To earn advanced degrees of their own and themselves
Become physicists and mathematicians and engineers—
Some scholars of history and philosophy and literature—
I have taught them well; though in truth nothing
Beyond to read carefully and to think for themselves
And trust their own minds. If I have taught them anything
It is to look beyond the seductive but elusive *why*
And keep their minds fixed firmly on *how* the world
Is ordered. Besides these simple truths there is no more
Exalted prescription for learning: that is merely the hype
Of hucksters and confidence-men bent on power and profit,
Or themselves bewildered and amazed at their own ignorance
And lack of understanding. Compared to such slick promises
This other way seems too simple—how is it something
So easy could work? Clearly it is not easy. Yet year after year
The young people have come and then gone away
To become scientists and scholars and artists. I have taught
Them very little, I think. Yet I have taught them well.